HOW DO THEY HELP?

COMMUNITY CONNECTIONS

COAT-A-KID

CHARITIES STARTED BY KIDS!

BY MELISSA SHERMAN PEARL AND DAVID A. SHERMAN

Published in the United States of America by Cherry Lake Publishing
Ann Arbor, Michigan
www.cherrylakepublishing.com

Reading Adviser: Marla Conn MS, Ed., Literacy specialist, Read-Ability, Inc.

Photo Credits: Photos used with permission from Coat-a-Kid, Cover, 1, 9, 11, 15, 17, 19, 21; © kikovic / Shutterstock.com, 5; © Blend Images / Shutterstock.com, 7; © Africa Studio / Shutterstock.com, 13

LIBRARY OF CONGRESS CATALOGING-IN-PUBLICATION DATA HAS BEEN FILED AND IS AVAILABLE AT CATALOG.LOC.GOV

Cherry Lake Publishing would like to acknowledge the work of The Partnership for 21st Century Learning. Please visit *www.p21.org* for more information.

Printed in the United States of America
Corporate Graphics

HOW DO THEY HELP?

CONTENTS

NEVER BE TOO COOL FOR SCHOOL

On any November day in St. Louis, Missouri, the daytime temperature is around 50 degrees Fahrenheit (10 degrees Celsius). Often it's colder. At night it can be in the 20s F (below zero C). As winter hits, the temperature drops even further and can reach 0°F (–17.8°C).

One chilly November afternoon in 2001, 9-year-old Maddy Beckmann

Having warm winter clothes is important if you're going to be outside.

ASK QUESTIONS!

In what kind of climate do you live? Is it warm or cold? Do you like snow? Would you prefer a different climate? Ask your friends and family about their favorite kind of weather.

came home from school with one thing on her mind: her coatless classmate. Maddy told her mom, “Why doesn’t she have a coat? She needs a coat.”

Betsey, Maddy’s mom, replied, “What do you want to do?”

After some thought, they bought a coat, hat, and gloves. The next day, they brought it to the school counselor so they could **anonymously** give the student the coat. The counselor told them that many kids didn’t have coats.

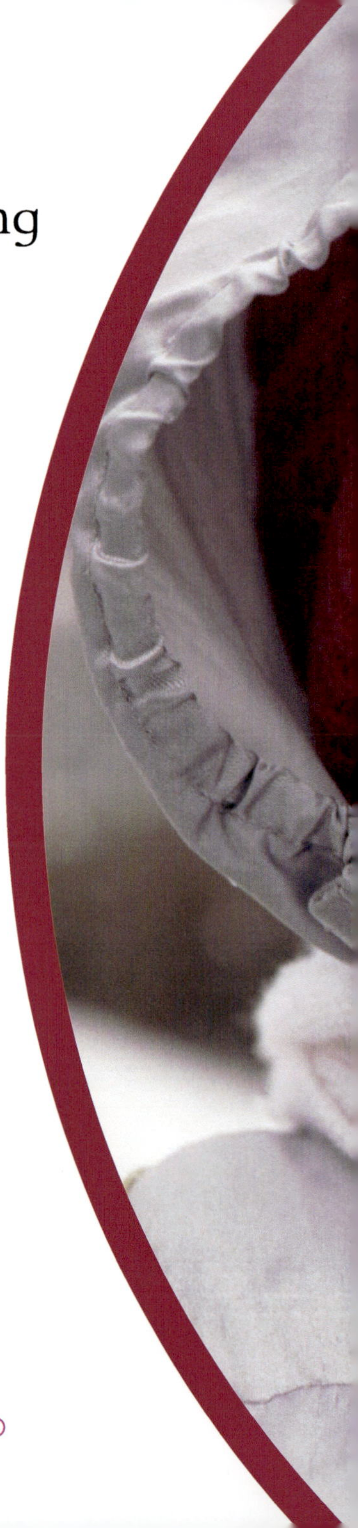

Many kids who don’t have warm coats also get free meals at school. If it’s too cold for those kids to get to school, they may not get lunch that day.

THINK!

Maddy and her mom donated the coat, hat, and gloves to her classmate anonymously. What does that mean? Why do you think that was important?

They discovered there were hundreds of children in St. Louis who did not have winter coats. Sometimes these kids couldn't go to school because it was too cold to wait at the bus stop.

The Beckmanns knew they had to do something. They added a new tradition to their annual Christmas cookie-decorating party. They asked guests to donate a gently used coat or a new hat and gloves. They collected 37 coats that year, and Coat-A-Kid was born.

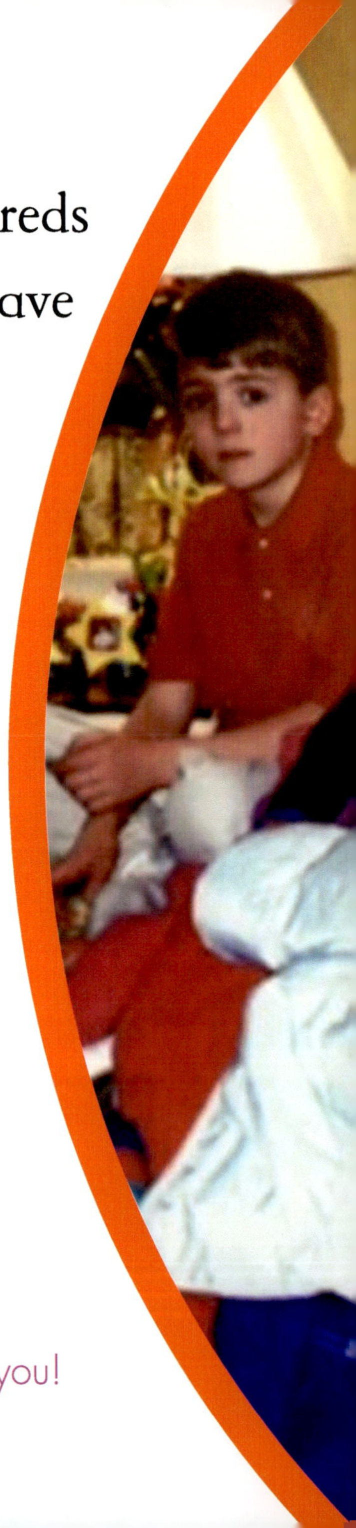

Coat-A-Kid started with a great idea from a kid like you!

MAKE A GUESS!

What season do you think the most people make donations in? If you guessed that the most people make donations around the holidays, you're right! Why do you think that is?

FINDING COATS—AND KIDS TO BE COATED

Maddy and her family started calling school counselors to find out who needed coats and at what schools. They focused on kids who were in the free meal program. By mid-January, those 37 coats had found homes.

Betsey started taking some of their grocery budget and buying coats. The Beckmanns also reached

With a warm coat, kids can get to and from school in the winter safely.

MAKE A GUESS!

If Coat-A-Kid has provided coats for more than 30,000 kids in 15 years, about how many kids is that per year?

out to friends and relatives for gently used or new coats. People held coat drives at their churches and schools. Unfortunately, much of it was unusable because it was either stained, way too big for kids, or not warm enough.

In 2005, they became a **nonprofit** organization. They could collect money to buy new coats, hats, and gloves.

As a nonprofit, Coat-A-Kid brought in more volunteers.

Nonprofit organizations collect money and volunteers to help those in need.

LOOK!

Because it is a 100 percent volunteer-run nonprofit, the only things Coat-A-Kid pays for are coats, hats, and gloves. Even its warehouse was donated. What kinds of expenses do you think other nonprofits have? Look online or at the library to find out.

The volunteers shop for bargains on terrific coats, hats, and gloves. On "coating days," they bring the coats (with matching accessories) and sort them by size and color for the kids. Because a child is more likely to wear something they like, they get to pick whichever coat catches their eye. The volunteers help make sure the coats fit right.

Maddy noticed that kids feel pride in having a nice, new coat of their own.

LOOK!

Many children who receive coats from Coat-A-Kid do not have heating where they live. They use the coats like a blanket to stay warm at home. Look online or at the library to find other ways they can keep warm at home. Maybe you can discover a new or underused energy source.

WARM HEARTS, EVEN WARMER KIDS

Since 2001, Coat-A-Kid has "coated" more than 30,000 kids. It now provides coats for all the kids, from ages 2 months to 4 years, in the YWCA and Urban League Head Start programs, as well as for elementary-age kids up to sixth grade. With the help of school social workers, volunteers drop off coats for homeless middle and high school kids,

Coat-A-Kid also provides coats for kids in the Angels' Arms foster care program.

THINK!

Volunteers with Coat-A-Kid purchase coats in many different colors and styles. Why do you think this might be important to the kids who receive the coats?

too. They also give coats to all the kids (ranging from a few months old to 18 years old) in the Angels' Arms foster care program—about 40 to 50 per year.

Coat-A-Kid is a totally volunteer-run organization without any paid employees. The legal and **accounting** services are provided **pro bono**. Postage stamps are the only other expense outside of the clothing.

Betsey remains actively involved and is president of the nonprofit's board

Maddy is still passionate about the nonprofit world, even though she's now a young adult.

ASK QUESTIONS!

John Henry Beckmann composed and recorded the music that Coat-A-Kid uses for the slide show presentation it sends to potential donors. Do you play any instruments? Do your friends or family? Talk to them about what kind of music they like to play.

of directors. Maddy graduated from Bryn Mawr College in Pennsylvania in 2015.

Coat-A-Kid believes that keeping kids in school is an important step toward ending the poverty cycle. It also knows that keeping kids warm is one more way to get them to school. Its motto is "Coat-A-Kid . . . because every kid deserves a coat."

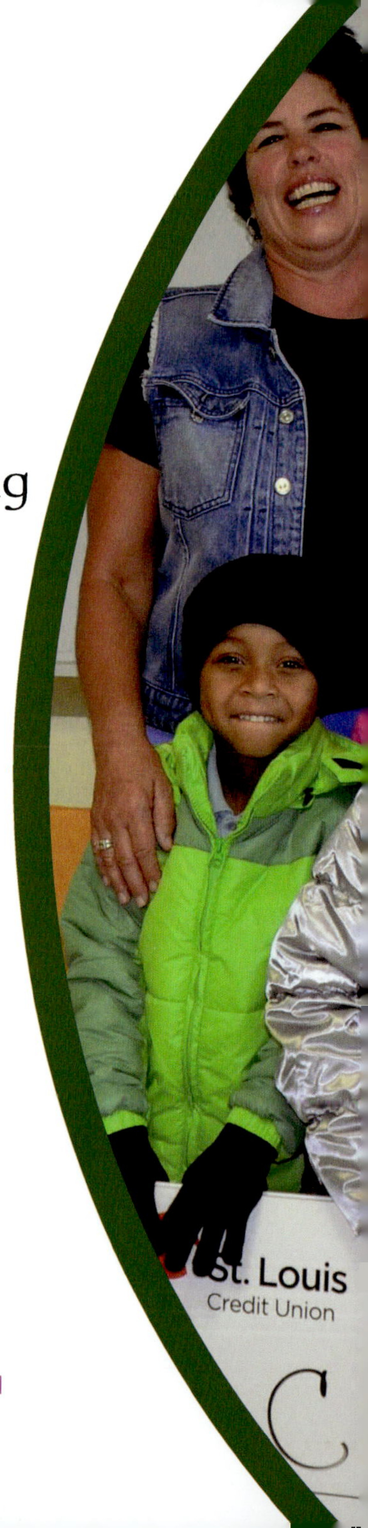

Coat-A-Kid has also given coats to janitors, cafeteria workers, and grandmothers in their community.

CREATE!

Caroline Beckmann created the Coat-A-Kid logo when she was 8. Create a new logo for your favorite organization and show it to someone there. See if the group would be interested in using it.

GLOSSARY

accounting (uh-COWN-ting) the practice of recording the amounts of money made and spent by a nonprofit or business

anonymously (uh-NAH-nuh-muhs-lee) without any name acknowledged

nonprofit (nahn-PRAH-fit) an organization that uses its money for charitable causes

pro bono (PROH BOH-noh) work done for free, generally for the public good

FIND OUT MORE

WEB SITES

http://angelsarms.org
Angels' Arms provides homes for foster children in St. Louis, Missouri, by keeping brothers and sisters together within a nurturing family until a permanent home is found.

www.coatakid.org
Learn more about Coat-A-Kid and what it does.

https://eclkc.ohs.acf.hhs.gov/hslc
Head Start promotes school readiness of young children from low-income families through local programs and services.

INDEX

ABOUT THE AUTHORS

David Sherman and Melissa Sherman Pearl are cousins who understand and appreciate that you don't have to be an adult to make a difference.